FLOWERS
AND
OTHER
FLAGRANCIES

FLOWERS AND OTHER FLAGRANCIES

POEMS

BY

LEAH

PARANSKY

LINTEL

LINTEL

Box 34 St. George Staten Island, New York 10301
and
430 Walnut Avenue S.E. Roanoke, Virginia 24014

ACKNOWLEDGMENTS

All titles in this book have been taken from *The Language Of Flowers*, a dictionary of the traditional meanings of flowers, published in England by Michael Joseph Ltd. Some of the poems have previously appeared in the following journals and anthologies: *Haiku Highlights, The Green World, Magic of the Muse, Cathedral Poets II, Cornucopia, Cimarron Review, Stepping Stones, Tracings of the Valiant Soul, The Picture Window, Lyrical Voices, Ever, Never, and Sometimes.*

CONTENTS

EGLANTINE . . .
Poetry, I wound to heal

CIRCAEA . . . A spell

you look
and I am
no longer
free

but am
that thing
you see
in me

BEGONIA . . .
Dark thought

I pare away
the bitter part
and wonder

will anything

be there when
I am through

BLACK POPLAR . . .
Courage

you lost your
baby boy
in Vietnam
and put on
Estee Lauder
lipstick and
crawled your
heart uptown

CONVOLVULUS, PINK . . .
Worth sustained by judicious and tender affection

<pre>
wrap   do not tie
enfold me
if you bind
please understand
one twist
of the cord
& love dies
by your hand
</pre>

NARCISSUS, DOUBLE . . .
Female ambition

volcanoes erupt
battles flare
women
wonder
what to wear

MEADOWSWEET . . .
Uselessness

to-fro
red-green
stop-go
fetus in womb
on wheels
I wallow away
my life
in automobiles

CEDAR LEAF . . .
I live for thee

a leech
never
sucks a
healthy
skin

TEASEL . . . Misanthropy

I didn't wish you
a happy birthday
not because I forgot
but because I don't
give a damn
whether you're happy
or not

DAFFODIL, GREAT YELLOW . . .
Chivalry

O our Guinevere
needs
shining deeds
there have been
no dragons
for years

PENNYROIL . . . Flee away

I would go away
anywhere   until Spring but
Spring would come too soon

AURICULA, SCARLET . . .
Avarice

bloated
abundance
doomed us
to consume
and consume
'til
consuming
consumed us

LAURESTINA . . . A token

I knit a shawl
for therapy
with all best
wishes
I present
this token of
my discontent

COLTSFOOT . . .
Justice shall be done

tulips
will strike
by the middle
of May and
wild flowers
will riot
in the cities
they say

CRAB BLOSSOM . . .
Ill nature

stranger I can
look   at you
which is more
than I can say
of those I see
every day

TREFOIL . . . Revenge

to avenge wrongs
we do not deliver
hot coals
with kid gloves

we use steel tongs

MIMOSA . . . Sensitiveness

my skin was thin
so I borrowed one
from a bear
I wear the thing
with daring pride

but there's more here
than meets the hide.

FROG, OPHRYS . . .
Disgust

poised
over me
in
nightly
rutting
ritual
you might
well be a
frog

WILLOW HERB . . .
Pretensions

I begged my books
one word of sustenance
from your vast store

in leathered array
they stood their shelf
and one by one refused
claiming vengeance for
the day oh fool I used
them for display

CANDYTUFT . . .
Indifference

poems collide
in my head

should they
demolish
each other

I would not
bear witness

BELVEDERE . . .
I declare against you

to be talked at
without looking
same
as walking away
I'd rather you
looked
without talking
when you have
nothing to say

LOTUS LEAF . . .
Recantation

I renounced pain
and joy also ended

ROSE, WHITE (WITHERED) . . .
Transient impression

clothes seedy & out of style
he is buying some one
a costly white rose which he
chose with a priceless smile

LARKSPUR, PINK . . .
Fickleness

lovers
are like mom's
old flat irons
it isn't cheating
to pick up one
while the other
is heating

ALMOND . . .
Stupidity, indiscretion

words
totally
hollow

not fit
for you
to eat

nor for
me to
swallow

MANDRAKE . . . Horror

our numbers will
continue to rise
and our progeny
will be reduced
to ant-like size
comparable to us
as we are
to the unlamented
dinosaur

WORMWOOD . . .
Absence

cold spot
in my thigh

ice cubes
in my heart

zero in July

next time
Hotshot
that we part

APPLE THORN . . .
Deceitful charms

I wish they
would leave
soon
before they
discover
the squirm
beneath
the croon

CONVOLVULUS . . .
Bonds

nor
can all tales
of all Gonerils
yet define
the prevailing wail
of the blood
protesting *mine*

CAMOMILE . . .
Energy in adversity

you teach the sun to shine
on your trailing onion vine
and tease potato eyes to sprout
and put them on the window sill
to shut the squalor out

ROSE LA FRANCE . . .
Meet me by moonlight

I walked by your house last night
lingered on the lawn
clambered up the balustrade
and peeked beneath your window shade
to prove that I am right when I insist
that angels do exist

POLYANTHUS, CRIMSON . . .
The heart's mystery

how our love fastens on a rag
a warped weave of rotten thread
and would you believe
the thing
hangs to-gether
and hangs us
by the heart
until we are dead

AFRICAN MARIGOLD . . .
Vulgar minds

you fill
the room
with
emptiness
crowding
me into
the corner
of myself

NEMOPHILA . . .
I forgive you

let sins
not fester
nor with
forgiving
indulgence
be sealed

better
let sins
be healed

BUGLOSS . . . Falsehood

the emperor mused
nude is merely bare
those fools out there
know I wear no clothes
and do they suppose
I can not see
their naked hypocrisy

VERNAL GRASS . . .
Poor but happy

I love
these wild weeds   these
pests with no pretensions
no striving after elegance
no aping of their betters
ah free they are
as I might be   were it not
for my fleshly fetters

SPEEDWELL, SPIKED . . .
Semblance

bats by day hang limp like rags
by day in trees in Katmandu bats
by day limp in trees in Katmandu
how do I dare and yet I do   com-
pare them hanging there   to you

HORTENSIA . . .
You are cold

I lie by your barred door
the thrust   is to love
the longing   is to trust

ah but that   is another
poem

MOSS . . . Maternal love

selflessly
I nurture
that you
may live
and love
and then   my own
you will come
owing an old crone
a bone

PERIWINKLE, BLUE . . .
Early friendship

when I was three
my partner in the
pat-a-cake bakery
shoved me off the
roof   that is how
I learned friends
are not necessar-
ily malice-proof

ORCHIS . . . A belle

no grand balls   to be belle of
no soaring romances to tell of
nor ever again
fond glances from men
ah the most invisible   of roles
is one for whom the belle tolls

ROSE, CHRISTMAS . . .
Relieve my anxiety

        pray let my
        roses die in
        their own bed
        I hate it
        when for a whim
        they have been
        mutilated

NIGHT BLOOMING CEREUS . . .
Transient beauty

        if I were twenty
        I too would dance till dawn

        ah my lady so briefly fair
        the grave lies yawning
        god knows no dancing's there

SPANISH JASMINE . . .
Sensuality

you make of love love love
a romantic spectacle and
never fail to avail yourself
of her as a receptacle

.

CROCUS . . .
Youthful gladness

your smile is a gorgeous thing
playful   mild   until it beams
& then it goes completely wild
a smile   bursting at the seams

ACACIA . . . Chaste love

were you to be smitten
with some ardent swain
who tells you that sex
has nothing to do with
the love myth
you had better find out
what he thinks
it does-with

CARDAMINE . . .
Paternal error

> have I visited upon you
> so venomous a blight
> that you choose
> to blossom and grow far
> from my relentless sight

FORGET-ME-NOT . . .
True love

> I send you
> flowers
> I picked them
> & pressed them
>
> tiny petals
> wistful prayer
> they are
> forget-me-nots

AMERICAN LINDEN . . .
Matrimony

who bore your babies
and kept your castle
for thousands of years or more
and how dear heart do you manage
to make her feel like a whore

GARDEN CHERVIL . . .
Sincerity

a gesture
will suffice
a nicety

who expects
for daily fare
so great
a rarity
as a sincerity

CHERRY TREE . . .
Good education

he spoke in accents
of a cultivated mind

and dined
in his undershirt
slurping coffee
with the spoon
stuck straight up
in the cup

FLOWERING REED . . .
Confidence in heaven

bodies strewn
in bloodied mud
to stare
with blackened
sightless eyes
at the blue
promise of heaven

ADONIS . . .
Sorrowful remembrance

chauffeur-driven cars
Mary-Annie-Cindy maids
food   parties   friends
WPA
and dad's lung cancer
mum's headaches from the
factory where she worked
and her saying all she
wanted was to go where
dad was and lie down under
a cover of closing twilight

CALEOLARIA . . .
Keep this for my sake

your gait your pace
for sure your posture
I took your place
time stalks its due
you can not hear
when I say   look dad
I walk like you

PRICKLY PEAR . . . Satire

a bird nest swings
in menacing winds
and I sing
how I sing
the freedom
of natural things

DEAD LEAVES . . .
Sadness

leaves that once
in youthful mirth
dallied with the sky
now lie as you   as I
mouldering
in death-giving earth

OATS . . .
The witching soul of my piano

I severed and slashed and clawed
stood in ruin up to my knees
suddenly all of the wood was gone
and there in mid-air hung the keys

BEE OPHRYS . . . Error

I'd never have believed
a bee could be deceived

this morning one dozes
on artificial roses

ICE PLANT . . .
Your looks freeze me

from high upon a rock
an eagle mocks
my earth-bound way
keeping his distance
with tacit insistence
that I keep mine   he
roots me   to the spot

FLAX . . . Fate

rarely
are we
to
ourselves
revealed
how mold
a destiny
so blind
so bound
so sealed

AURICULA . . . Painting

no mere
resemblance
I swear

my children
to the bone
& the artist

eerily
to me
unknown

AGNUS CASTUS . . .
Coldness

framed in elm trees
smiling at the night
through windows
veiled in pale gauze
ah a house it was
that posed
while doors inside
against each other
closed

NARCISSUS . . . Egotism

I talked and talked
the whole night through
and made my charms
felt by you
you made no replies
but lay transfixed
adoring me with your eyes
on and on I charmed
until the daylight
crawled upon our bed
and I saw you were dead

COLCHICUM . . .
My best days are over

old clock old crone
long years of time
you've watched
my hurrying
beloved old thing
you no longer chime
& I no longer sing

LUCERNE . . . Life

spin
little spider the web of your life
in musty corners of a room
your whole world could go you know
with the swish-swish of a broom